RAGS

HERO DOG of WWI

A True Story

By Margot Theis Raven

Illustrated by Petra Brown

WAR DOGS of WWI

The First World War began on July 28, 1914, and ended on November 11, 1918. Battles took place in more than eight different areas of the world and on three continents. Of all the major fighting armies, only the United States did not formally make dogs a part of its WWI military ranks, but Germany (with 30,000 dogs), France and England (with 20,000 each), and other countries trained Canines Corps to be sentry, messenger, and ambulance dogs. There was another kind of historic canine-soldier called the mascot dog.

These unlikely soldier-dogs were strays who usually attached themselves to a person or combat unit and ended up going to war beside the humans they "adopted." Although not initially militarily trained, these dogs were gratefully utilized by U.S. forces in WWI. They bravely risked their lives and lifted the spirits of battle-weary troops. Their story is an old one. It began when a dog first befriended man. And man was the better for it.

Many, many years ago during WWI, there lived a real dog who began life in an alleyway of a Paris café. The dog was a shaggy mutt, a small, scrappy gutter-pup, who belonged to no one but the streets where he roamed. He didn't even have a name except for the angry ones café owners yelled to chase him from their garbage. The stray lived by his wits alone, for he hadn't a friend in the world since the day he was born.

Then one July evening sirens blared. They warned the people of Paris to shutter windows and black out lamps so they wouldn't be seen by enemy planes. Danger filled the streets, so the dog took shelter in an empty doorway just as the night turned dark as a pocket. The mutt didn't know his life was about to change when an American soldier stumbled in the inky blackness and —YIPE! — stepped on his paw.

The soldier lit a match and saw a scraggly face with two worried eyes staring at him. "Did I hurt you, pal?" asked Private James Donovan. He'd come with the U.S. Army's Fightin' First Division to help France end the war. Donovan picked up the mutt. The dog had never been held before and he liked the feeling, until a stern military policeman appeared.

"Your pass," the policeman demanded of Donovan.

"Sure hope you're a good-luck pup," Donovan whispered to
the dog, because he didn't have a pass that allowed him to
be out in the city at night. He had marched in a big Paris
parade that day with an American battalion. Instead of
returning to base, Donovan had stayed in Paris to sightsee.
Now he was in trouble.

"Sir, this dog is our division mascot. I ran off base to find him when he went missing. Our unit pulls out tomorrow, and our commander wouldn't be happy to leave this little guy behind." Donovan quickly made up a tale taller than the Eiffel Tower!

"Dog? He looks like dirty rags to me," scowled the military policeman.

"Yes, sir!" Donovan agreed. "That's exactly how he got his name. First Division Rags. Quite the pup he is!"

The policeman nodded. The name sure fit. He decided to let them go.

Back at the army base, Rags sat still and straight by Donovan's side in front of the commander. A surprised Private Donovan learned that instead of being in trouble, he'd gotten a new rank and assignment that very day.

"Pack up, sergeant, tonight you move out for the battlefield," the commander told him.

"Rags, too, sir?" hoped Donovan.

"Rags, too," the commander agreed. "He seems a smart fellow."

Rags and Donovan rumbled out of Paris in a motor truck.
"Good ol' Rags," Donovan said, scratching the dog's head.
"We're in this war together now." Rags curled up by his side.

Rags stayed close to the soldier. Even when Donovan tried to keep him from the battlefront, Rags jumped out a window at the division headquarters and followed him in secret.

Back at camp, Donovan felt a wet nose nudge him. It was Rags. From that day on, he was Donovan's dog through thick and thin.

Rags liked infantry work, especially sharing Donovan's food rations and drinking water from his helmet. Rags found many important jobs to do.

He chased mice and rats out of the field trenches where the soldiers slept and ate.

His ears heard the buzz of incoming shells before the soldiers did. When Rags fell belly-to-dirt, the soldiers did too. Rags loved rolling in the dirt. It made his shaggy eyebrows look like fuzzy caterpillars to Donovan.

Rags even learned to salute. He'd raise a paw to his face, then drop it as a smart show of respect. Once a general walked by. Rags stopped, squatted, and raised a paw.

The general respectfully returned his paw.

Donovan was a signalman. He laid telephone wires on the
ground so soldiers at the battlefront could communicate
with soldiers in the rear, the ones with the biggest guns.
Rags's nose read Donovan's wires like a book, and he helped
him find breaks in the lines.

Rags worked as a runner, too. Donovan would put a piece of paper under Rags's collar, turn him to face the rear, and say, "Go find!" Rags then ran toward the sound of the big guns and waited there until someone came to take his message. It was his most dangerous job.

Donovan made Rags a little gas mask to protect him from the enemy's poisonous gas. Rags hated it. It blocked his nose; he couldn't smell. He'd push it off with his paws, but Donovan would put it right back on. "We don't want you going west on us, pal," he'd say in the way soldiers spoke of dying. Rags didn't understand Donovan, but his voice calmed him like a nap in the sun. So he'd keep the mask on.

By late September of 1918, news about the hero mascot had spread throughout the First Division. Soldiers told how Rags had bitten an enemy's leg to defend Donovan ... how he'd crawled under barbed wire to run messages ... and how he never gave up, not for a minute, no matter how much the sky exploded.

He became a legend of courage. A giant of a dog.

Then one day, October 9, 1918, a major battle began in Argonne Forest. Fog was so thick Donovan couldn't see his lines. The air was choked with poison. Men were trapped. Donovan tightened their gas masks and tied a message on Rags. It told the rear soldiers where to fire to help the men.

Donovan's mouth was tight with worry as he gave Rags the command, "Go find." Rags began the run back when a big blast hit nearby. It sprayed metal like hard rain over Rags.

It cut his paw, his ear, his eye. It threw Donovan to the ground, tore off his mask. Rags's mask was gone, too. He licked Donovan's face. Donovan struggled to his feet. They moved together. Donovan and Rags, limping, staggering toward the rear. Another shell hit.

It flipped Rags to the ground.

A soldier found him and the message he carried.

Wounded Donovan was taken to a field hospital. "Rags?"
he gasped as he awoke to find his dog beside him.

Then loudly, the big guns began to fire! **CRASH, BOOM**...
blasted the shells from the rear to rescue the trapped men. Rags
turned his face up to Donovan at the good sound. He knew.

"You did it, pal!" Donovan's smile broke wide over Rags.
"You saved them."

In the field hospital, a doctor found Rags under Donovan's blanket. He took a shell splinter from Rags's eye, sewed up his ear and foot. One ear was deaf, one eye blind. He'd limp.

But Rags was alive and with his Donovan.

Donovan's friend hid Rags under his coat to board the dog on a hospital ship taking Donovan to America. Base hospital staff in Chicago cared for Donovan. Rags had healed. He lived in the firehouse on base. Rags made a bed for himself under the hose cart but spent each day with Donovan. He'd sit outside the main hospital door in the morning and wait for someone to let him in. Then he lay on Donovan's bed, being good medicine, until he had to leave at dusk.

One day in the hospital, Donovan wrapped his arms around Rags. "Good ol' Rags," he nuzzled against his neck. Rags sensed Donovan put a "Go Find" message under his collar with the hug. But no paper was there. Donovan grew weak from coughing that day, so Rags licked his hand.

The following morning, Rags was frantic when he couldn't find Donovan. He searched the ward bed by bed. Exhausted with worry, he went to the front door. Paced. A medical officer knew Donovan was in critical care, a place for very ill soldiers. "I'll get you to him tomorrow, I promise," he told Rags.

Rags left the hospital. No tail wagged.

And Donovan died in the night.

The next day, the medical officer took Rags to Donovan's empty bed. "The pup needs to learn in his own way," he'd convinced the hospital staff.

Rags lay down where Donovan wasn't anymore. His nose read the story of Donovan's last day. Donovan's lungs were tired. He was cold. He had gone west for a nap in the sun.

Rags stayed on the bed for a long time that day. Then he climbed off. He walked the hallway to the front door for the last time and waited for the medical officer to open it. He wagged his thanks. Then Rags walked slowly to the firehouse.

It is told that Rags never went near the hospital again. He knew Donovan wasn't there.

His best friend now lived in his heart.

EPILOGUE
Donovan's Message

Rags was sad in the spot that wagged his tail. He missed Donovan. And so he grieved, but Rags wasn't alone. The First Division mascot had a family now, a military family, and a forever home in the U.S. Army.

Then one day, Major Raymond W. Hardenbergh moved on base with his wife and two young daughters, Helen and Sue. Rags *just knew* in the spot that wags the tail that he had a message for them from Donovan! Not a paper one, but a "Go Find" note just the same. It came with Donovan's last hug. It said: please love my dog. Rags wanted the girls to find it, but they grew wary of his friendly barks. So Rags stopped. He remembered when carrying a "Go Find" note, he had to wait until *someone found him*.

Helen and Sue knew Rags was a hero. Rags showed them he was a good dog, too. The girls took Rags into their house one day. Soon the Hardenbergh home became his, but when Major Hardenbergh was assigned to a new base, the family learned Rags could not go with them! As an army member, Rags was an official ward of the base. Helen and Sue pleaded to army officials.

The officials ruled the Hardenberghs could have trusteeship of Rags—for his best good! Still, the girls were told if Rags wished to stay where he had last lived with Donovan, it was his choice. The family packed up and piled in the car, but the girls left the car door open and waited.

Rags wanted to go and wanted to stay; then he remembered a doorway in Paris that had changed his life forever. Donovan would want him to jump through this one. He did. Rags leapt into the car between the two girls. And rode into his many happy years ahead.

THE *Tail* END 🐾

On March 21, 1936, Lt. Col. Hardenbergh released a statement that Rags had died at 20 years of age. The news ran in the *New York Times*. Rags's obituary told he was some kind of pup! He was part mutt, part cairn terrier (Toto in the *Wizard of Oz* was of the cairn breed). The hero dog served in three major WWI campaigns and saved many lives. For his bravery he received two service chevrons (awards), two wound chevrons, a U.S. Army decoration, and he was inducted in the Legion of Hero Dogs. The Long Island Kennel Club also created a dog show category (with ribbon awarded) for his outstanding wartime accomplishments.

Newspapers, magazines and a biography (placed in the Imperial War Museum in London) covered Rags's lifetime achievements, such as when he led the WWI 10th Anniversary Parade down Broadway in New York City. He was photographed with the attending legendary WWI generals.

Rags lived with the Hardenbergh family on several military bases. At Fort Benning, Georgia, Rags was badly injured when hit by a car while crossing the street. His blind eye and deaf ear made street crossing difficult. With typical pluck, Rags battled back to wander again.

Rags lived his last years in Washington, D.C., where John J. Pershing, the supreme commander of the U.S. Army Forces in France, gave First Division Rags a ride one day.

Rags is buried at Aspen Hill Park in Silver Spring, Maryland. His tombstone reads:
RAGS, War Hero, 1st Division Mascot WWI, 1916 – 1936.

But to Donovan, Rags was the loyal little dog who made The Great War human.

*To my dog-loving mother, who knew a "fur child" puts a smile on your face, and
to my grandchild Asher, who always puts a smile on my face.*

Margot

★

For Iain
Petra

★

AUTHOR ACKNOWLEDGMENT

Thank you to the National World War I Museum
at Liberty Memorial, Kansas City, Missouri.

FOR FURTHER READING

RAGS: The Story of a Dog Who Went to War written by Jack Rohan,
originally published in 1930 by Harper & Brothers

★

Sleeping Bear Press®
315 E. Eisenhower Parkway, Suite 200
Ann Arbor, MI 48108
www.sleepingbearpress.com

Printed and bound in the United States.

10 9 8 7 6 5 4 3 2 1

Raven, Margot Theis.

Rags : hero dog of WWI : a true story / written by Margot Theis Raven ;
illustrated by Petra Brown.

pages cm.

Summary: "A stray dog named Rags befriends a U.S. soldier in Paris, France,
during WWI. Rags traveled with the troops carrying messages from the front line
to the back. His loyalty kept him by his owner's side until Sergeant Donovan
died at the base hospital in Chicago"— Provided by the publisher.

ISBN 978-1-58536-258-5

1. Rags (Dog) 2. World War, 1914-1918—Dogs. 3. Dogs—War use—United States—
History—20th century. 4. Working dogs—United States—Biography. 5. Donovan,
James, -1919. 6. World War, 1914-1918—Regimental histories—United States—
Infantry Division, 1st. I. Brown, Petra, illustrator. II. Title.

D639.D6R38 2014

940.4'12730929—dc23   2014004557